Spot the Shape

Comparing Shapes

Charlotte Guillain

www.raintreepublishers.co.uk
Visit our website to find out more information about Raintree books.

To order:

☎ Phone 0845 6044371

🖹 Fax +44 (0) 1865 312263

🖥 Email myorders@capstonepub.co.uk

Customers from outside the UK please telephone +44 1865 312262

Raintree is an imprint of Capstone Global Library Limited, a company incorporated in England and Wales having its registered office at 7 Pilgrim Street, London, EC4V 6LB – Registered company number: 6695582

Raintree is a registered trademark of Pearson Education Limited, under licence to Capstone Global Library Limited

Edited by Rebecca Rissman, Charlotte Guillain and Catherine Veitch
Designed by Joanna Hinton-Malivoire
Picture research by Tracy Cummins and Heather Mauldin
Originated by Dot Gradations Ltd
Printed in China by Leo Paper Group

ISBN 978 0 431 19394 6 (hardback)
13 12 11 10 09
10 9 8 7 6 5 4 3 2 1

ISBN 978 0 431 19400 4 (paperback)
14 13 12 11 10
10 9 8 7 6 5 4 3 2 1

British Library Cataloguing in Publication Data
Guillain, Charlotte
Comparing shapes. - (Acorn plus. Spot the shape)
516.1'5
A full catalogue record for this book is available from the British Library.

Acknowledgements
We would like to thank the following for permission to reproduce photographs: ©Alamy pp. 9 (EggImages), 11 (Stefan Sollfors), 14 (Tetra Images), 15 (Anne-Marie Palmer), 19 (Gary Cook), 22c (Anne-Marie Palmer); ©Getty Images pp. 7 (Chung Sung-Jun), 8 (DAJ), 12 (Helifilms Australia/Contributor), 16 (William Huber), 22b (DAJ); ©Jupiter Images pp. 5 (Comstock), 10 (Royalty Free Corbis), 18 (Judith Rosenbaum); ©Shutterstock pp. 4 (Ryan van Graan), 6 (Jip Fens), 13 (Lance Bellers), 17 (Andreas G. Karelias), 22a (Jip Fens), 22d (Andreas G. Karelias).

Front cover photographs reproduced with permission of ©Getty Images/Panoramic Images. Back cover photograph of a window in a building reproduced with permission of ©Jupiter Images (Royalty Free Corbis). Back cover photograph of Zulu bead work reproduced with permission of ©Alamy (EggImages).

Every effort has been made to contact copyright holders of material reproduced in this book. Any omissions will be rectified in subsequent printings if notice is given to the publishers.

Contents

What is a shape?. 4

Circles. 6

Triangles 8

Squares 10

Rectangles. 12

Ovals 14

Semicircles 16

Diamonds. 18

Comparing shapes 20

Describing shapes 22

Shapes to know. 23

Words to know 23

Index 24

Notes for parents and teachers 24

Some words are shown in bold, **like this.** They are explained in the "Words to know" section on page 23.

What is a shape?

There are many different shapes in the world around us.

Some shapes have straight lines and **corners**.

Some shapes have **curved** lines and no corners.

Some shapes have many **sides**.

Some shapes have one side.

Shapes can be large or small.

Circles

A circle is a round shape with one **side**.

Can you draw a circle?

We can see circles in many different places.

Can you spot a circle?

Triangles

A triangle has three **sides** and three **corners**.

Can you draw a triangle?

We can see triangles in many different places.

Can you spot a triangle?

Squares

A square has four **sides** and four **corners**.

All of a square's sides are the same length.

Can you draw a square?

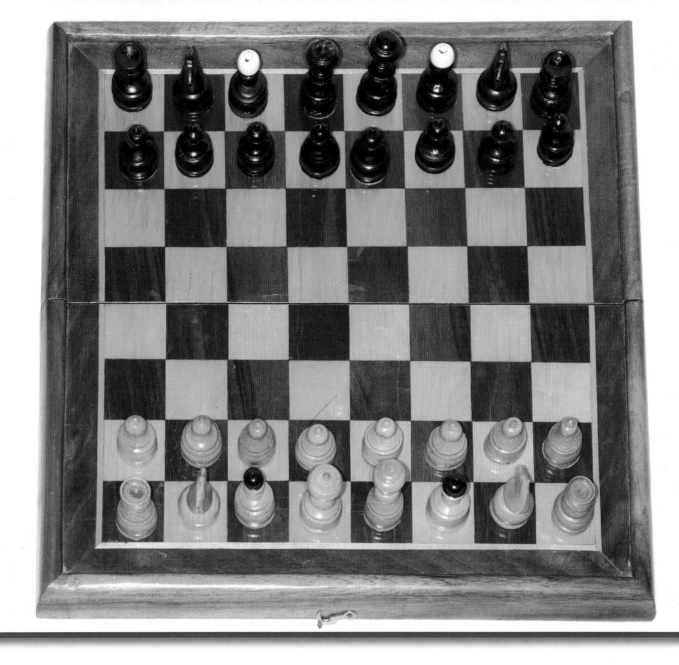

We can see squares in many different places.

Can you spot a square?

Rectangles

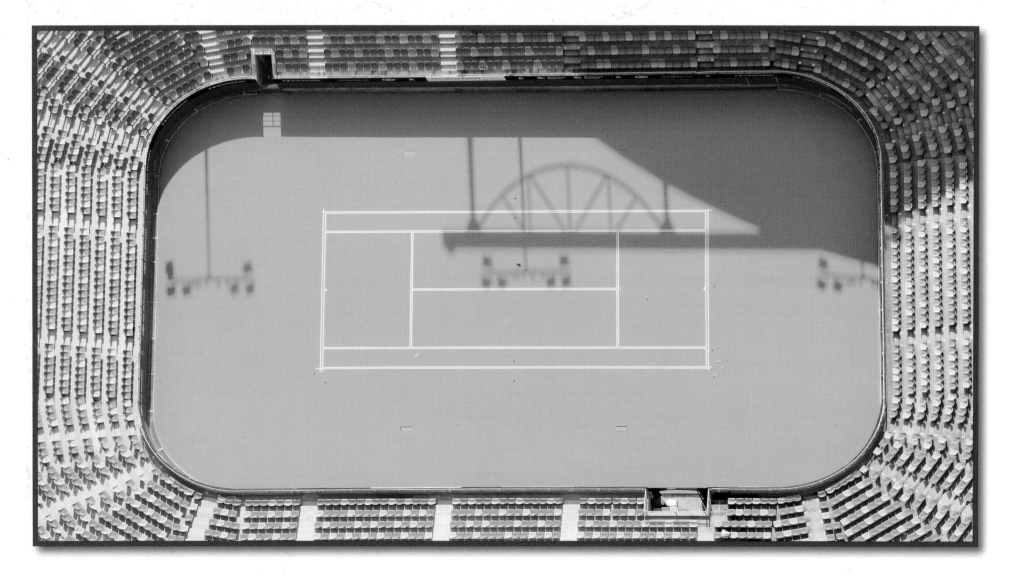

A rectangle has four **sides** and four **corners**.

Two of the sides are longer than the other two sides.

Can you draw a rectangle?

We can see rectangles in many different places.

Can you spot a rectangle?

Ovals

An oval is like a squashed circle. It is **curved** and it only has one **side**. Can you draw an oval?

We can see ovals in many different places.

Can you spot an oval?

Semicircles

A semicircle is **half** a circle.

It has a **curved side** and a straight side.

Can you draw a semicircle?

We can see semicircles in many different places.

Can you spot a semicircle?

Diamonds

A diamond has four **sides** and four **corners**.

Can you draw a diamond?

We can see diamonds in many different places.

Can you spot a diamond?

Comparing shapes

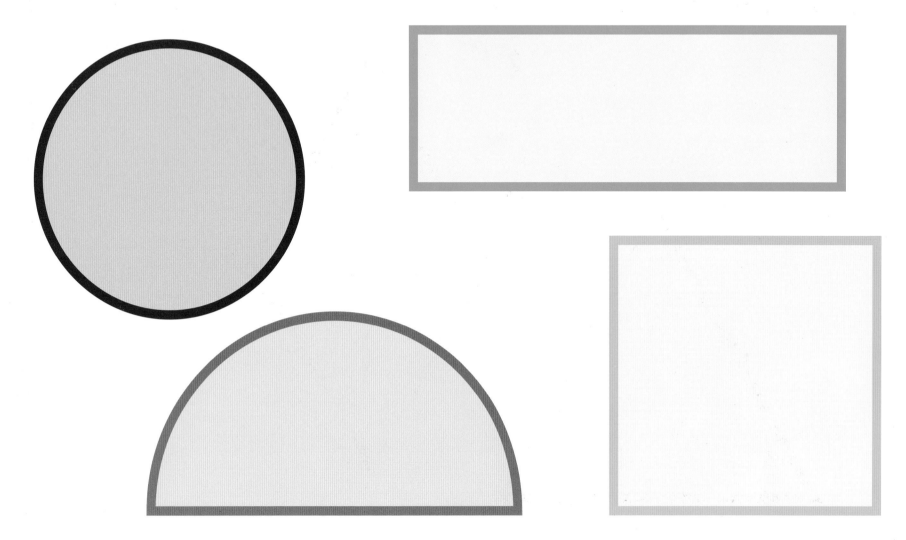

How many of these shapes have **curved sides**?

How many of these shapes have **corners**?

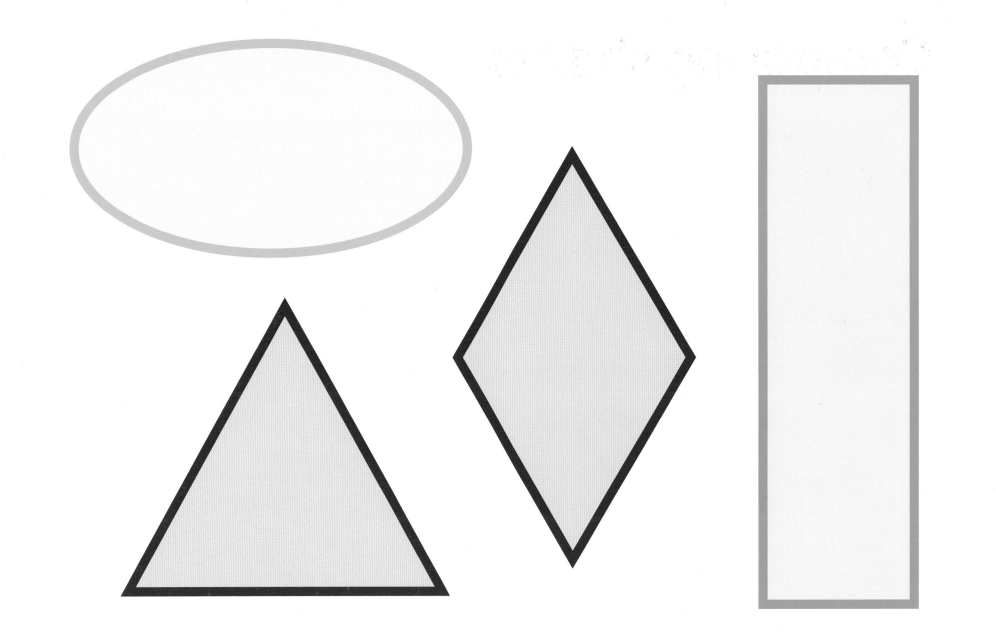

How many of these shapes have four sides?

How many of these shapes have three sides?

Describing shapes

How many **sides** and **corners** do these shapes have?

What are these shapes called?

Shapes to know

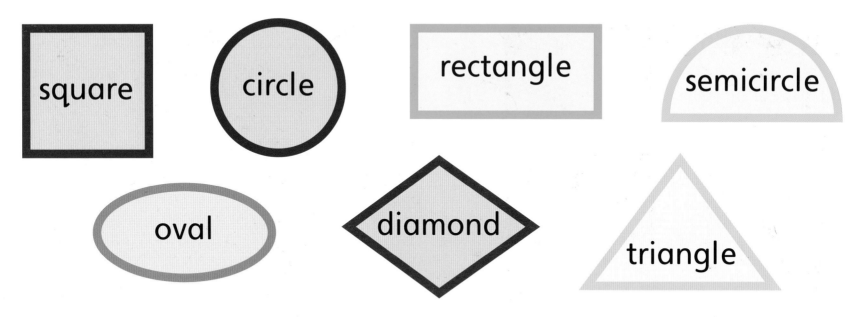

square circle rectangle semicircle

oval diamond triangle

Words to know

compare	put two or more things together to show how different or similar they are
corner	place where two lines or edges meet
curve	line that bends
equal	of the same size
half	one of two equal parts that together make up the whole of something
side	part at or near the edge of something

Index

circle 6, 7, 23

diamond 18, 19, 23

oval 14, 15, 23

rectangle 12, 13, 23

semicircle 16, 17, 23

square 10, 11, 23

triangle 8, 9, 23

Notes for parents and teachers

Before reading

Make a set of the shapes shown on pages 20 and 21 out of card. Hold up each shape in turn to the class and ask the children what it is called. Hold up two shapes at a time and ask the children questions. For example, hold up the circle and the oval and ask how these shapes are the same or different, hold up the square and the rectangle and ask how these shapes are the same or different.

After reading

• Snap: draw three sets of the following shapes on card: squares, rectangles, diamonds, circles, ovals. Shuffle the cards and share out between two children. Each child takes it in turns to turn over a card. If both shapes have the same number of sides then the first child to shout "Snap!" wins a counter. Continue until one child has 10 counters.

• Shape doodle: draw a shape in the air with your index finger. Ask the children to copy your shape. Draw a shape in the air with your other index finger, making it a mirror image of the first shape you drew. Challenge the children to do the same.

• Shape sort: put four hoops on the floor and label each hoop with the following labels: 0 sides, 1 side, 2 sides, 3 sides, 4 sides. Then shuffle the shape cards you made earlier and ask the children to place the cards in the correct hoop. Play the game again, labelling the hoops with 0 corners, 1 corner, and so on.